Contents

Who Is Miranda Cosgrove?

Miranda Cosgrove is a television and movie actress. In 2003, the film *School of Rock* put Miranda in the spotlight. She was only nine years old when she won the role of band manager Summer Hathaway in the movie.

A few years later, Nickelodeon created a television show for her called *iCarly*. The show quickly became popular. Today, more than 11 million viewers watch *iCarly* each week. The show has helped Miranda become one of the highest-paid teen actresses in Hollywood.

Miranda's bubbly personality attracts fans from around the globe. She is a regular on the covers of magazines such as *J-14* and *Twist*.

"It's probably the weirdest when I go to the mall or out to eat with my friends, and a bunch of people will come up and be excited about the show—that's when I start to realize,'Wow, I'm on a show, and people watch it."

REMARKABLE PEOPLE

Miranda Cosgrove

by Anita Yasuda

MEDIA ENHANCED BOOKS

AV2 BY WEIGL

ADDED VALUE • AUDIO VISUAL

www.av2books.com

AV² provides enriched content that supplements and complements this book. Weigl's AV² books strive to create inspired learning and engage young minds in a total learning experience.

Your AV² Media Enhanced books come alive with...

Audio
Listen to sections of the book read aloud.

Key Words
Study vocabulary, and complete a matching word activity.

Video
Watch informative video clips.

Quizzes
Test your knowledge.

Embedded Weblinks
Gain additional information for research.

Slide Show
View images and captions, and prepare a presentation.

Try This!
Complete activities and hands-on experiments.

... and much, much more!

Go to www.av2books.com, and enter this book's unique code.

BOOK CODE

B 7 4 4 4 3 6

AV² by Weigl brings you media enhanced books that support active learning.

Published by AV² by Weigl
350 5th Avenue, 59th Floor
New York, NY 10118

www.av2books.com   www.weigl.com

Library of Congress Cataloging-in-Publication Data

Yasuda, Anita.
  Miranda Cosgrove / Anita Yasuda.
    p. cm. -- (Remarkable people)
  Includes index.
  ISBN 978-1-61690-668-9 (alk. paper) -- ISBN 978-1-61690-673-3 (pbk. : alk. paper)
  1. Cosgrove, Miranda, 1993---Juvenile literature. 2. Actors--United States--Biography--Juvenile literature. 3. Singers--United States--Biography--Juvenile literature. I. Title.
  PN2287.C634Y38 2011
  791.4302'8092--dc22
  [B]
                        2010051144

Printed in the United States of America in North Mankato, Minnesota
1 2 3 4 5 6 7 8 9 0 15 14 13 12 11

WEP37500
052011

Editor: Heather Kissock
Design: Terry Paulhus

Photograph Credits
Weigl acknowledges Getty Images as the primary image supplier for this title.

Every reasonable effort has been made to trace ownership and to obtain permission to reprint copyright material. The publishers would be pleased to have any errors or omissions brought to their attention so that they may be corrected in subsequent printings.

Growing Up

Miranda Taylor Cosgrove was born on May 14, 1993, in Los Angeles, California. She grew up just outside Los Angeles in the city of Downey. Her mother, Chris, stayed at home to care for Miranda. Her dad, Tom, owned a dry cleaning business. Miranda has no brothers or sisters.

Even as a young child, Miranda loved to perform. In 1996, a three-year-old Miranda went out to dinner with her parents. Instead of eating her meal, Miranda started singing. One of the other diners in the restaurant was a talent **agent**. He told Miranda's parents that Miranda could be a child model. The agent offered to help Miranda find modeling and acting jobs.

■ Miranda started acting at an early age.

Get to Know California

FLOWER
Golden Poppy

TREE
Redwood

MAMMAL
California
Grizzly Bear

Oregon
Idaho
Nevada
Utah
California
Arizona
USA
MEXICO
N

0   200 Miles
0   200 Kilometers

Mount Whitney is the highest point in California. It is 14,495 feet (4,418 meters) above sea level. It is also the highest point in the United States outside of Alaska.

Created in 1958, the Hollywood Walk of Fame honors excellence in the entertainment industry. Joanne Woodward received the first star in 1960. Today, there are more than 2,000 stars.

The Academy Awards are held in Los Angeles every year. The awards honor the best in the movie industry.

Sacramento is the capital of California.

Think about it!

Today's celebrities have very little privacy. Media coverage about their lives is constant. Think about how hard it would be to maintain your privacy. Some stars, such as Miranda Cosgrove, manage to stay out of **tabloids.** How do you think this is possible? What measures could you take to lead as normal a life as possible?

Practice
Makes Perfect

With her agent's help, Miranda was soon getting parts in commercials and print advertisements. Miranda liked the process of making commercials. She enjoyed playing a part and meeting new people. By the time she was seven years old, she knew she wanted to be an actress.

When Miranda was eight years old, she landed her first television acting job. It was a small part on *Smallville*. One year later, Miranda **auditioned** for the Nickelodeon comedy *Drake & Josh*. It starred actors Drake Bell and Josh Peck. Miranda won the role of troublemaker sister Megan.

■ *Drake & Josh* won the 2006 Nickelodeon Kids' Choice Award for Favorite Television Show.

At about the same time, Miranda was awarded the role of Summer Hathaway in *School of Rock*. Miranda quickly packed her bags and flew to New York to make the movie. After the movie's release, the cast of the movie, including Miranda, was **nominated** for Best On-Screen Team at the MTV Awards and Best Young Ensemble in a Feature Film at the Young Artist Awards.

Miranda continued to attract attention as a young actress. Her next role was in the movie *Yours, Mine and Ours* in 2005. Following this movie, she was again part of a nomination for Best Young Ensemble in a Feature Film at the Young Artist Awards.

■ Miranda attended the Los Angeles premier of *Yours, Mine and Ours* with some of her cast mates.

Key Events

Miranda has worked steadily since she was three years old. Over time, she has been offered different types of acting jobs. Her initial roles in commercials led to television roles, and then to movies. She gained a reputation for being a hard-working actor.

Her acting on *Drake & Josh* caught the attention of television **executives**. They decided that Miranda should have her own television show. She was given the starring role in *iCarly*, which **debuted** in 2007. The show was a hit from the beginning. *iCarly* became the highest rated program in its time slot for children ages 2 to 11.

iCarly has also helped Miranda begin a singing career. In 2007, she sang on the **soundtrack** for the show. She followed this with her own **album**, Sparks Fly, in 2010.

■ *iCarly* is about a girl who hosts a Web show. The show is taped in a television studio in Los Angeles.

Thoughts from Miranda

Miranda has worked hard to become a successful performer. Here are some comments she has made about acting, singing, and her life.

Miranda talks about her first album.

"I've been co-writing and getting really into it. It's still pop-rock fun music like the *iCarly* soundtrack, but I think it's a little more mature."

Miranda talks about why *iCarly* is popular.

"...this is really the first TV show with Internet, and kids can really interact with it."

Miranda talks about her fans.

"I really think it's cool when I go to the mall, and kids come up to me and say the episodes they like and talk to me about how much they enjoy the show."

Miranda talks about her plans for the future.

"I want to go to college, and I want to keep acting and singing. I love entertaining people and making them laugh. It's my favorite thing to do."

Miranda gives advice to people wanting an acting career.

"Just to keep trying and not give up, because I have a lot of friends that are actors that try out for auditions, and it's just all about getting the part that's right for you, so sometimes it takes a while."

Miranda compares acting in movies and on television shows.

"...with movies, it's fun, because you get to travel [to] different places and stuff like that, and plus it doesn't take as long. But I love being on a TV show because you get to know the people so well, just from seeing them every day."

What Is an Actor?

Actors are people who play the roles of characters in dramatic productions. They use their speech, body language, and movement to pretend to be other people. The stage, radio, television, and movies all provide opportunities for actors to perform.

Actors work long hours. As their jobs are irregular, some also work other jobs. Often, actors must learn lines and movements that are written in **scripts**. Sometimes, actors do not use a script. They say and do what they feel in the moment. This is called improvisation.

In order to play different roles, actors need to have talent and experience. Usually, actors train at acting schools or work with a drama coach to improve their skills. They take classes on voice and **diction**.

■ Miranda has learned how to act through on-the-job training.

Actors 101

Shenae Grimes (1989–)

Shenae began her acting career when she was a teenager. Her first movie was about country singer Shania Twain. Shenae played a young Shania. Her next big break came when she landed the role of Darcy Edwards on the television series *Degrassi: The Next Generation*. When the show *90210* was being developed, Shenae signed on to play the character of Annie Wilson.

Ashley Tisdale (1985–)

Ashley is an actor, singer, and television producer. At the age of three, Ashley met her agent at a shopping mall. She then began acting in television commercials. Ashley became very well-known after being cast in the series *The Suite Life of Zack and Cody*. Later, she played Sharpay Evans in Disney's *High School Musical*. Ashley has since gone on to star in both *High School Musical* sequels and has released two albums.

Blake Lively (1987–)

Blake was born in Tarzana, California. In 2005, she tried out for a movie called *The Sisterhood of the Traveling Pants*. She won the role of Bridget Vreeland. This led to more roles in movies and television. In 2007, she landed the role of Serena van der Woodsen on the television show *Gossip Girl*. The role has brought her many awards, including the 2008 Teen Choice Award for Choice TV Actress: Drama and the Choice TV Breakout Star: Female.

Keke Palmer (1993–)

Keke is an actor and singer. She began her film career in *Barbershop 2: Back in Business*. Next, she appeared in television dramas such as *ER* and *Cold Case* and the movie *The Wool Cap*. She then went on to win an NAACP award for her starring role in the movie *Akeelah and the Bee*. In 2007, she released her R&B album *So Uncool*. Keke is currently the star of her own show on Nickelodeon, *True Jackson, VP*.

The Birth of Television

People first had the idea of transmitting sounds and pictures in the late 1800s. It took about 50 years to develop the technology to capture images with a camera and send them to a screen. Regular television broadcasting did not begin in the United States until the late 1940s. Some of the first television shows were boxing matches and game shows.

Influences

Miranda is close to her parents, Chris and Tom. They help Miranda make career decisions by going through scripts together. While they support her acting dreams, they have never pushed their daughter. This has helped Miranda stay grounded.

One of Miranda's favorite actors is Rachel McAdams. Rachel, like Miranda, began acting at a young age. Anne Hathaway is another actress whom Miranda admires. Like Miranda, Anne worked in television. She then moved into film, where she became well known for her role as Mia Thermopolis in *The Princess Diaries*.

■ Rachel McAdams starred in *The Notebook*. This is one of Miranda's favorite movies.

Both Anne and Miranda have worked as **voice actors**. Anne was in the animated feature *Hoodwinked*, and Miranda was in *Despicable Me*. Miranda provided the voice for a cookie-selling orphan who is adopted by evil mastermind Gru, voiced by Steve Carell.

Miranda is a big fan of Judd Apatow's movies, including *Forgetting Sarah Marshall*. Judd produces and writes comedies. Miranda appreciates the humor that his movies have. She would like to do more comedy because she enjoys entertaining people and making them laugh.

THE COSGROVES

Miranda Cosgrove lives in Los Angeles with her family. She and her parents are very close. Her parents have tried to keep Miranda's life as normal as possible. She has to do chores and keep her room clean. Her parents have encouraged her to go to college as well. She hopes to attend university in New York and study film.

■ The film program at New York University is considered one of the best in the world.

Overcoming Obstacles

Miranda's rise to being one of the highest-paid teen actresses has not been without challenges. Miranda auditioned for many parts she did not get. Although disappointed, Miranda remained positive. Other jobs soon came her way.

School is important to Miranda, but so is acting. For a long time, Miranda tried to balance school and work. It soon became too confusing going back and forth between them. Miranda made the decision to leave formal schooling behind. She started working with tutors. Later, she began taking her courses through an online school.

■ As an actress, Miranda travels quite often. She has to go where her project is being filmed, and she has to travel to promote the film when it is done. Her travels have taken her across North America.

Taping a hit show is hard work. Actors have to work long hours. Some days, they are at the studio before sunrise. There, they have to attend several rehearsals. They also have to be available for the planning of lights and cameras. Sometimes, Miranda is required to stay late on set. This can be tiring for her. With support from family and friends, however, Miranda stays focused. This allows her to do quality work.

■ Miranda sometimes spends extra time at work showing guests around the set for *iCarly*.

Achievements and Successes

Miranda has been nominated for several acting awards in her short career. In 2007, she was nominated at the Young Artist Awards for Best Performance in a TV Series (Comedy or Drama) by a Supporting Young Actress for her role as Megan Parker. Two years later, she won the Leading Young Actress award for her role in *iCarly*.

While working on her TV show, Miranda sang professionally for the first time. She recorded the show's theme song, "Leave It All to Me." Miranda had so much fun that she wanted to go back to the studio. *iCarly*, the soundtrack from the show, debuted at number 28 on the **Billboard** charts in June 2008.

■ Miranda appeared on the *Today Show* to promote her album.

Miranda spent the next two years working on her full-length recording debut. She co-wrote many of the songs on the album. Released in 2010, Sparks Fly peaked at number eight on the Billboard album charts.

Miranda ended 2010 on a high note. Not only was her debut album in the top 10, her show *iCarly* won the Kids' Choice Award for Favorite TV Show.

HELPING OTHERS

Often, actors use their popularity to increase public awareness about issues they care about. They may bring attention to nonprofit organizations, environmental causes, or help fund special causes. Miranda is involved with the Afterschool Alliance. The program provides resources to about 26,000 after-school programs across the United States. Miranda supports this group because she remembers how important being in after-school programs, specifically baseball, was to her.

Write a Biography

Aperson's life story can be the subject of a book. This kind of book is called a biography. Biographies describe the lives of remarkable people, such as those who have achieved great success or have done important things to help others. These people may be alive today, or they may have lived many years ago. Reading a biography can help you learn more about a remarkable person.

At school, you might be asked to write a biography. First, decide who you want to write about. You can choose a actor, such as Miranda Cosgrove, or any other person. Then, find out if your library has any books about this person. Learn as much as you can about him or her. Write down the key events in this person's life. What was this person's childhood like? What has he or she accomplished? What are his or her goals? What makes this person special or unusual?

A concept web is a useful research tool. Read the questions in the following concept web. Answer the questions in your notebook. Your answers will help you write a biography.

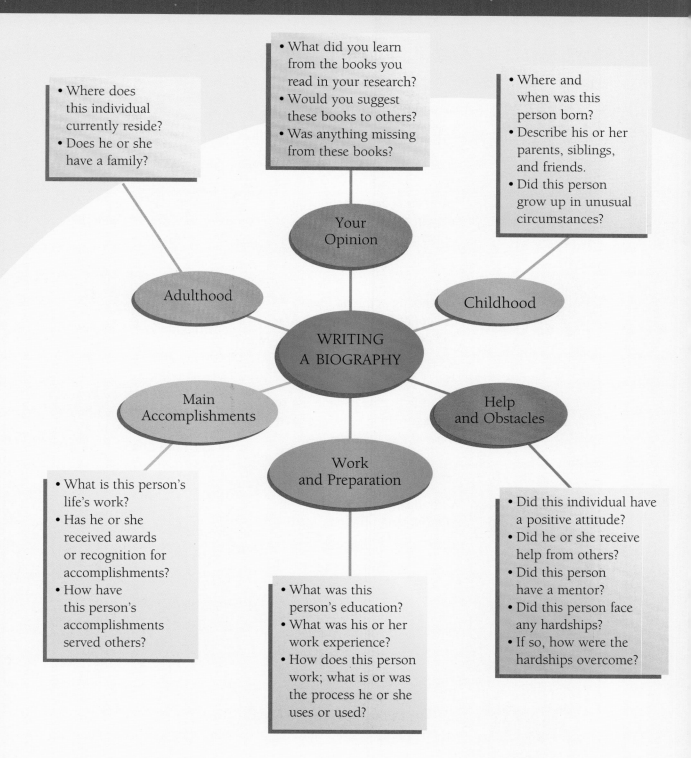

- Where does this individual currently reside?
- Does he or she have a family?

- What did you learn from the books you read in your research?
- Would you suggest these books to others?
- Was anything missing from these books?

- Where and when was this person born?
- Describe his or her parents, siblings, and friends.
- Did this person grow up in unusual circumstances?

Your Opinion

Adulthood

Childhood

WRITING A BIOGRAPHY

Main Accomplishments

Help and Obstacles

Work and Preparation

- What is this person's life's work?
- Has he or she received awards or recognition for accomplishments?
- How have this person's accomplishments served others?

- What was this person's education?
- What was his or her work experience?
- How does this person work; what is or was the process he or she uses or used?

- Did this individual have a positive attitude?
- Did he or she receive help from others?
- Did this person have a mentor?
- Did this person face any hardships?
- If so, how were the hardships overcome?

Timeline

YEAR	MIRANDA COSGROVE	WORLD EVENTS
1993	Miranda is born in Los Angeles, California on May 14.	*Jurassic Park* is released and becomes the highest-**grossing** film made at that time.
1996	Miranda is discovered while singing at a restaurant in Los Angeles.	*Ace Ventura: When Nature Calls* wins Favorite Movie at the Kids' Choice Awards.
2003	Miranda is in the hit film *School of Rock* with Jack Black and Joan Cusack.	The one billionth song is downloaded on iTunes.
2004	Miranda begins playing the role of Megan on the Nickelodeon show *Drake & Josh*.	*Harry Potter and the Prisoner of Azkaban* wins the Choice Movie- Drama/Action Adventure at the Teen Choice Awards.
2005	Miranda stars in *Yours, Mine and Ours* with Dennis Quaid and Rene Russo.	Carrie Underwood wins *American Idol*.
2007	Miranda lands the lead in the Nickelodeon show *iCarly*.	*High School Musical 2* becomes the most watched made-for-cable movie.
2010	*iCarly* wins the Kids' Choice Award for favorite television show.	Taylor Swift releases her third album.

Words to Know

agent: a person who finds performers for the entertainment industry and helps performers find jobs that suit their skills

album: a collection of songs released in one package, such as a CD

auditioned: performed to try to get a job in the entertainment industry

Billboard: charts produced by a weekly magazine that rate the popularity of music

debuted: made a first appearance

diction: pronouncing words properly and clearly

executives: people who run large companies

grossing: total sales

nominated: added to a small list of people who will be considered for an award

scripts: the written text of plays, movies, or television shows

soundtrack: music from a movie or a television series

tabloids: celebrity and gossip magazines

voice actors: people who provide the voice for animated characters

Index

Log on to www.av2books.com

AV² by Weigl brings you media enhanced books that support active learning. Go to www.av2books.com, and enter the special code found on page 2 of this book. You will gain access to enriched and enhanced content that supplements and complements this book. Content includes video, audio, web links, quizzes, a slide show, and activities.

Audio
Listen to sections of the book read aloud.

Video
Watch informative video clips.

Embedded Weblinks
Gain additional information for research.

Try This!
Complete activities and hands-on experiments.

WHAT'S ONLINE?

 Try This!

Complete an activity about your childhood.

Try this activity about key events.

Complete an activity about overcoming obstacles.

Write a biography.

Try this timeline activity.

 Embedded Weblinks

Learn more about Miranda Cosgrove's life.

Learn more about Miranda Cosgrove's achievements.

Check out this site about Miranda Cosgrove.

 Video

Watch a video about Miranda Cosgrove.

Check out another video about Miranda Cosgrove.

EXTRA FEATURES

 Audio
Listen to sections of the book read aloud.

 Key Words
Study vocabulary, and complete a matching word activity.

 Slide Show
View images and captions, and prepare a presentation.

 Quizzes
Test your knowledge.

AV² was built to bridge the gap between print and digital. We encourage you to tell us what you like and what you want to see in the future.

Sign up to be an AV² Ambassador at www.av2books.com/ambassador.